The Almost Adventures of Plane Jane

Written by

Aja Dorsey Jackson

Illustrated by Jasmine Mills

Charm City Press
2019

For Kya

Copyright © 2019 by Charm City Press
All rights reserved. This book or any portion thereof may not be reproduced or used in any manner whatsoever without the express written permission of the publisher except for the use of brief quotations in a book review.

Printed in the United States of America

First Printing, 2019

ISBN: 978-1-7339205-1-3

Ordering Information:
Quantity sales. Special discounts are available on quantity purchases by corporations, associations, and others. For details, email the publisher at books@charmcitypress.com.

This is the story of a girl named Jane
Who set off to take a ride in her bright blue plane.
Jane and her plane took to the sky
And this is the tale of how she knew
She could fly.

Grandma's house is where the story begins.
Jane lived there near all her friends
With daddy, and mommy, and Kelsey, and Clay
And a park nearby where she loved to play.

Until one day…

Jane, Mommy, Daddy, Kelsey, and Clay
Hopped onto a truck and moved far, far away!

They moved to a house on Mulberry Circle
With a great big backyard
And a porch trimmed in purple;
With shiny new floors
And two big garage doors,
Four beds, three baths, and much, much more.

"This brand new place is a great big bore,"
Said Jane as they rode in the car to the store.
"I miss the house on Taylor Street
And getting around on our own two feet.
Now, everything is way too far.
All we ever do is ride around in the car."

Daddy said: "Now, Jane, please give it a while.
Think nice thoughts and try to smile."
But she couldn't think nice and was feeling too down
So Jane sat with a frown as she rode around town.

But next Sunday would be super fabulous.
Sundays were when they would have the most
Delicious dinner that grandma would make-
Mac and cheese, steak and greens, and pineapple cake.

"Sunday's the day for Gram's mac and cheese!
We have to go have some!
Please, mommy, please!"

"Grandma's house is too far away.
We'll have to go another day.
But if you want, here's what I'll do.
I'll make that mac and cheese for you."

"Uhhh....no thanks, mom, yours isn't the same.
(And I might add, just a *little* bit lame.)"

Jane thought she might begin to cry
Until she lifted her eyes high
And found an answer in the sky.

"I know, I'll fly!"

"No one will let you on a plane all alone."

"That's okay; I'll just build my own."

"What kind of kid can build a plane?
I mean, think of it, Jane,
It's a little insane.
Fly in the sky?
That will never work.
I'm pretty sure you've gone berserk."

But, you see, that Jane was pretty smart
And with a little bit of math
And science
And art
Jane knew that she could fly in the sky.

Jane worked on her plane all day and night.
She knew if she gave it all her might
She'd research and draw and build just right
And Jane and her plane would soon take flight.

Sunday arrived! Her day was here.
Time to put that plane in gear.
Jane pulled on the handle of her plane just so.
But try as she might, the plane just wouldn't go.
Jane sighed. Oh no.

"I've worked too hard to give up now.
I'll get this plane to fly somehow."

She hit that plane, and it made a sound
So loud she had to turn around
And she couldn't believe her very own eyes.
To her surprise
It started to rise!

Out of Mulberry Circle, past the trees and beyond
Over Fern Valley School and Blueberry Pond.
Jane hopped on top of the warm wind's flow
As the shops and hilltops turned to spots down below.

Jane dashed and she flashed
and she zoomed through the sky.
"Here I come, macaroni and hot apple pie!"
And Jane, the fearless little flyer,
Tried to take her plane up even higher.

She pulled on the handle and gave it her all
But Jane and her plane
They started
To
Fall.

"Mayday! Mayday! Let's redirect!
My calculations were incorrect.
I think I'm running out of gas.
I need to land this plane-and fast!"

Jane quickly turned her plane around
And landed safely on the ground
Back at home, safe and sound.

"I did it! I did it!" Jane exclaimed
I flew through the sky in my very own—"

"Jane! Did you hear me calling your name?
Come on, come on, look who came!"

Grandma came! With food galore.
Mac and cheese, and a whole lot more.
Jane and her family sat down to eat
And having everyone together was her favorite treat.

"But Jane, your plane
didn't make it to the end!"

"I flew once and I'll fly again.
You'll see!
This brave and fearless girl
Will soon be flying
Around the world"

Where will Jane be flying next?
Visit us at planejanebook.com to learn more!

Did You Know....

Jane is inspired to fly by reading about leaders in aerospace! Learn more about some of Jane's inspirations.

Bessie Coleman was born in 1892 and was the first African American woman to hold a pilot license. Because African Americans and women were not allowed to be trained to fly in the United States at the time, Ms. Coleman traveled to Paris to earn her pilot license. She became a stunt flyer, performed daredevil tricks before audiences, and eventually became known as "Queen Bess" for her exhibition flying.

The Tuskegee Airmen were the first African American military pilots in the United States. They were officially formed in 1941 at Tuskegee University and went on to fight in World War II. The Airmen overcame segregation to become some of the best pilots in the U.S. Army Air Forces.

Guion "Guy" Bluford is the first African American to have gone to space. Mr. Bluford flew fighter planes for the U.S. Air Force and won many medals. He joined the NASA space program in 1978, and orbited the earth 98 times as part of member of the crew of the Orbiter Challenger in 1983.

Dr. Mae Jemison became the first African American woman to fly in space in 1992 when she served as a mission specialist aboard the Space Shuttle Endeavour. Dr. Jemison was a member of NASA's astronaut corps and orbited the Earth for nearly eight days in September 1992.

Information obtained from the Smithsonian National Air and Space Museum.

About the Author

Aja Dorsey Jackson is an author and editor from Baltimore, Maryland. She loves to doodle, daydream, and spend time with her three children. When she isn't doing any of those things, she is busy writing stories of all varieties. Her first children's book, *Shine*, was published in 2019.

Made in the USA
Middletown, DE
13 December 2019